YORKSHIRE COAST &
NORTH YORK MOORS
FROM ABOVE

FLIGHTIMAGES

Photographs: IAN HAY, FLIGHT IMAGES
Text: LISA PRITCHARD

MYRIAD BOOKS

North York Moors

The sheer scale of the openness of Yorkshire's moors can take your breath away. While much of the moorland is privately owned, extensive footpaths and rights of way ensure that the land is accessible to walkers, cyclists and horse-riders. Most of the region is in the North York Moors national park. Established in 1952, this is an area of outstanding natural beauty. It stretches from Danby at the head of the Esk Valley in the north to Pickering in the south. Together with open countryside and moorland, the region contains historic buildings such as the abbeys of Byland, Rosedale and Rievaulx, and historic houses such as Duncombe Park. The 110-mile (176km) Cleveland Way national trail begins on the eastern rim of the park at Helmsley and crosses its northern edge to join the coast at Saltburn where it follows the Heritage Coast south to Ravenscar.

GOATHLAND

Black-faced sheep still graze the village commons and the surrounding Goathland Moor, just as they have in past centuries. The village is scattered around a series of large greens which are common land. In the first half of the 20th century this land was also used as a golf course, with players driving the balls right across some of the roads in the village.

There has been an upsurge of tourists in recent years. Adults come to see the village where the popular television series *Heartbeat* is filmed, and children want to see the station where the Hogwarts Express arrives in the *Harry Potter* films.

The station, with two tracks, is one of the few places on the North Yorkshire Moors railway line where trains can pass. This is the longest steam railway line in England. The steam trains carry about 200,000 passengers a year through some of the most scenic Yorkshire moors, along 18 miles (29km) of track between Grosmont and Pickering.

DANBY

Towards the northern edge of the North Yorks Moors national park, Danby sits in a hollow near the head of the Esk valley. The village has a working water mill down by the river. Above the village is Danby Beacon, one of many hilltops where beacons were lit to warn neighbouring villages of invaders such as the Vikings. Danby Low Moor and, on the other side of the Esk Valley, Danby High Moor are common land which is administered by the Danby Court Leet. This original feudal court is still active and based at Danby Castle. Today the castle, built in the 14th century but now in ruins, is part of a working farm. Catherine Parr was Lady of the Manor here before she became Henry VIII's sixth wife. Danby benefits from a railway station and is a useful stop on the line from Middlesbrough to Whitby.

HELMSLEY

The full extent of the dramatic double ditch that formed the moat of Helmsley Castle is clearly visible in this photograph. The ditches were cut out of the rock on which the original castle was built early in the 12th century. Some years later the timber buildings were replaced with a stone curtain wall, round corner towers, a D-shaped tower halfway along the east wall and a portcullis in the south wall. Cromwell's forces besieged the castle for three months in 1644, and on its surrender much of the fortress was destroyed. The commander saved the west range, however, as a gift for his daughter. Behind the castle lies the market town of Helmsley.

DUNCOMBE PARK

This beautiful Italianate house with its pedimented attic stands on a plateau with views over Helmsley Castle and the river Rye. An amateur architect, William Wakefield, designed the main house. Building started in 1711 and service blocks were added either side of the sweeping drive in 1843. The house survived a major fire in 1879 and served as a girls' school for 60 years after the First World War. Today it is largely as originally designed, with landscaped gardens and parkland. On the east side, the exterior steps up to the hall, with its Corinthian half-columns, are complemented by the formal parterre gardens established in the 1840s and a particularly fine 18th-century terrace with circular classical temples.

BYLAND ABBEY

Eight miles west of Thirsk, and just two miles north of Rievaulx Abbey, the warm sandstone ruins of Byland Abbey stand as a testament to the Cistercian monks who founded a community here in the 12th century. From unpromising beginnings on a marshy, wooded site, the monks laboured to build one of the largest and most prosperous cloisters in England with a thriving sheep farm that exported wool. The community survived largely unaffected by politics and wars until the dissolution of the monasteries during Henry VIII's reign. The abbey's interior was stripped in 1537 and the buildings left to decay. In the 1920s preservation work began. You can still see traces of a huge rose window in the great sweep of the abbey's west front, while inside the south transept, the chapel's intricate and colourful tiled floors hint at the glories that were lost during the Reformation.

ROSEDALE ABBEY

This tiny village took its name from a small 12th-century Cistercian priory, of which there is little evidence today. The remaining stones were used to build the present village church in the mid-19th century. The quiet village you see now was very different during the Industrial Revolution when 5,000 men worked in the nearby ironstone mines. The old kilns and a chimney still stand as a reminder of this era.

WITTON FELL

The lush green lower slopes of Witton Fell peter out towards East Witton, a tiny village at the crossroads of two small country roads. This seems a sleepy village now but it was not always so. The A6108, one of the roads that passes through today, used to be the main route for coaches travelling from Kendal to York, and the coach drivers would have to slow down to avoid overturning as they tackled the dramatic right-angled bend in the village. In the distance stretches Braithwaite Moor. At its heart, seemingly far from anywhere, stands Braithwaite Hall, a 17th-century stone farmhouse with impressive panelling and an oak staircase. It is now owned by the National Trust.

SPAUNTON MOOR

The bleak stretches of Spaunton Moor lie between Rosedale Abbey and the village of Hutton-le-Hole. Famous today for grouse-shooting, the moor has many traces of human activity from past centuries, with disused mines and sheep trails. As you wander over the moor you are likely to come across tumuli, burial mounds from prehistoric times, and cairns, stones piled high as a memorial or to mark a boundary. The moor is dotted with numerous old wayside markers designed to guide travellers across the barren countryside. Hutton-le-Hole is a pretty village with a folk museum (British Museum of the Year in 1995), a blacksmith's shop, a thatched church and an historic schoolhouse.

FYLINGDALES

The name Fylingdales is inextricably linked today with the controversy surrounding the ballistic early warning system and its three huge golfball shaped radars that dominated the landscape in the 1960s and 1970s. These were replaced with a pyramid-shaped radar in the 1980s, but campaigners continue to protest against Fylingdales' enhanced role in the US missile defence system.

The moor itself, which is situated close to the A169 between Pickering and Whitby, has a bleak beauty and is popular with walkers in the summer. In winter, however, walkers are well advised to stay indoors when snow falls, as the drifting snow can catch all but the most experienced unawares and quickly engulf them. Fylingdales lies close to the Hole of Horcum, a huge natural amphitheatre hollowed out of heather-clad moorland and known locally as "The Devil's Punchbowl".

PICKERING

The Vale of Pickering runs from the cliffs near Scarborough, westwards to the Howardian Hills. Some 17 miles (27km) inland lies the market town of Pickering, on the banks of Pickering Beck. Pickering is the official gateway to the North York Moors national park and is a pretty contrast to the countryside to the north. The town's coat of arms shows a pike with a ring in its mouth. In 272BC a local king is said to have lost his ring in the river; later a cook found it in the belly of a pike fished from the water. The motte and bailey castle was first raised by William the Conqueror as a defence against marauding Scots. For three centuries kings of England would stay here and hunt in the surrounding forest, but from the 17th century onwards the castle was left to decay. The ghost of a tall monk clad in grey has been reported crossing the castle grounds to the keep. Beck Isle Museum is housed in a handsome Regency house near the town centre. Its 27 galleries give an insight into local life and customs.

KILBURN WHITE HORSE

Carved into Royston Scar in the Hambleton Hills overlooking the Vale of York, this giant white horse is something of a Victorian folly. Thomas Taylor, a master grocer, was very impressed by the White Horse carved into the hills at Uffington in Berkshire. In 1857 he recruited the village schoolmaster and 20 men to carve his own version, some 314ft/96m long and 228ft/69m high, into the hillside. However, unlike the chalk of the Berkshire hills, the land here is limestone, so the carving must be regularly whitened. Early on this was done with whitewash, but now chalk is brought in to coat the horse and keep it white. When the weather is clear, the horse can be seen from some 40 miles (64km) away, and walkers on the hill have a view all the way across the Vale of York to the city itself.

RIEVAULX ABBEY

In 2003 the restored ruins of this austere 12th-century monastery emerged from scaffolding after seven years of repairs. With Byland Abbey and Fountains Abbey, this was one of the three great Cistercian abbeys in Yorkshire. It was the base from which the Cistercians set out to establish monasteries in the north of England and Scotland. The abbey sits at the foot of a steep hill, so the monks had to build the church's aisle running north to south rather than the traditional east to west. The aisle walls are no longer standing, but the nave arcading and upper windows are still impressive.

Rievaulx is just two miles (3km) from Byland Abbey: it is said that the monks could not tell which abbey's bell was ringing to call them to prayer.

NEWBY HALL

The architect Robert Adam was commissioned to redecorate the interior of this beautiful house, built in 1695 during the reign of William and Mary. Adam created a domed sculpture room and a tapestry room to house the treasures that William Weddell brought back from his Grand Tour in 1765-6. Experts today consider this interior to represent the very best of Robert Adam. The house is built around a paved courtyard. Garden enthusiasts come to Newby Hall for the 25 acres (10ha) of gardens and the national collection of *Cornus* (dogwoods).

RIPON

The cathedral city of Ripon sits on the banks of the river Skell. At its heart is the market square, a mix of medieval and Georgian buildings. Every evening at nine o'clock the Wakeman blows a large curved horn in Ripon's market square. For over 1,000 years this tradition has been maintained; the Wakeman blows to reassure the citizens that they are safe for the night. Luckily not all Ripon's traditions have lasted as long: there used to be two sets of gallows in the town, and 300 people were executed in 1569. Today Gallows Hill is a housing estate and the city's name is more likely to be linked with the winner of the 3.45 at Ripon on one of its famous race days.

THIRSK

Thirsk's name dates from Viking times, and means "marshy place". It sits in the Vale of York, within a few miles of the North Yorkshire moors to the east and the river Swale to the west. Racegoers come to Thirsk's racecourse in the summer months for the flat racing. But there is more to this charming town, with its cobbled marketplace. Coaches disgorge their tourists here on the trail of the James Herriott stories, whose author Alf Wight lived and worked as a vet in the town. His surgery has now been converted into the Herriot Centre, laid out as it would have been when he practised there. A small independent cinema has entertained the locals for 90 years, and is now run by volunteers. The beautiful Perpendicular church of St Mary dates from the 15th century.

THORNBOROUGH CIRCLES

These dumbbell-shaped henges are the biggest Neolithic complex between Stonehenge and the Orkneys, and are one of the greatest and least understood ancient monuments in Britain. Exploratory digs have revealed graves and small household items such as flint knives. When seen from the air, the massive scale of the circles constructed 5,000 years ago starts to become apparent – the earthworks form part of a "sacred vale" that extends over 40 miles (64km).

NORTHALLERTON

Ideally placed for easy access to both the northern Dales and the North York Moors, this market town is the administrative centre of North Yorkshire. It sits at the centre of the Vale of York, 32 miles (51km) to the north-west of York. The busy high street is broad and about half a mile long. Towards the top of this photograph you can see the Early English church of All Saints, which is cruciform with a Perpendicular tower. A national newspaper judged the Christmas puddings made here by Lewis & Cooper to be the best in the UK in 2002. The company exports 4,500 puddings a year to the United States.

COD BECK

The Cod Beck river rises in Osmotherley Moor, and continues southwards down to the river Swale through the village of Osmotherley and the town of Thirsk. This reservoir was built, together with a water filter house in Osmotherley, in the 1950s to serve the Northallerton area. Periodically, Cod Beck reservoir is in the news as thousands of toads return every year to breed there. If the weather is good, this is a popular picnic spot, so the toads need to negotiate some busy roads to reach the water and return again after breeding. The reservoir is also the starting point for serious walkers undertaking the Lyke Wake Walk. This is a tough 24-hour challenge which takes the walkers across the centre of the moors to Ravenscar on the coast.

CATTERICK

From its early days as a Roman fort to the era of horse-drawn coaches, travellers on the Great North Road would stop overnight in Catterick to rest themselves and their horses. Today, the road is formally known as the A1 and most of the traffic rushes by. A key attraction of the village is the racecourse where flat and jump races are held throughout the year, as well as a huge Sunday market every week. Six miles (4km) to the north-west of Catterick Village and three miles (2km) from Richmond lies the British Army's largest base. The base has gradually incorporated the outlying villages of Colburn, Scotton and Hipswell and the resulting town has a population of 12,000 people.

THE COAST

THE SPECTACULAR COASTLINE of Yorkshire offers much to thrill the eye: dramatic cliffs with teeming birdlife, villages that seem to perch precariously on sheer precipices, miles of sandy beaches and the ever-changing North Sea.

The region's maritime legacy (with its most famous son, Captain Cook) and legitimate international trade were once matched by its reputation for smuggling, the craggy shorelines offering plenty of shelter from the excise men. The fishing industry remains an important factor in the local economy today.

Seaside resorts such as Scarborough and Filey retain their popularity as holiday destinations, attracting many thousands of visitors each year, while the city and port of Hull is an important industrial and commercial centre. The regeneration of this historic city was heralded by its newest visitor attraction – the gleaming glass and aluminium marine life centre named The Deep which was designed by Sir Terry Farrell and opened in 2002.

STAITHES *left and below*

Staithes hugs the southern headland of Penny Nab, while across the Staithes Beck the tiny hamlet of Cowbar lies high on Penny Nab. "Steers", as you will hear Staithes referred to locally, is considered one of the north-east coast's most picturesque fishing villages. Its brightly painted Whitby cobles, the region's fishing boats, can moor safely in Staithes harbour even during the worst of the sea's winter storms. In 1744 James Cook was taken on by the village draper as an apprentice; two years later he ran away to sea and eventual fame as Captain Cook. With the advent of the railway in the late 19th century, an artists' community sprang up; today the village is still popular with visiting painters.

RUNSWICK BAY

The coastal village of Runswick clings like a limpet to the foot of the cliffs on the west of Runswick Bay. With its sandy beaches it has been a haven for fishermen and whalers (and inevitably, smugglers) since Roman times. Today, however, there are few fishing boats left, and you are more likely to find tourists and fossil collectors strolling along the beach. The very shifting nature of the cliffs that makes them so rewarding for fossil hunters has, over the years, proved a problem for the inhabitants of the village. Extreme weather caused a catastrophic landslide in 1682, and the rebuilt cottages often suffered cracks during the centuries that followed, until a sea wall was built in 1970.

SANDSEND

No prizes for guessing what is Sandsend's best feature! The village sits at the northern end of a beautiful long sandy beach. At low tide you can walk under the cliffs north of the village exploring the rock pools with their tiny fish, crabs and anemones. In the shale on the foreshore you may find the occasional ammonite, or even an ichtyosaurus bone if you are lucky. In the early 1700s alum was quarried here to supply the tanning industry (it made leather supple and durable) and for fixing dyes in textiles. The excavations completely changed the cliff profile of Sandsend Ness, and the strange shapes of the mounds of debris now form part of the landscape.

WHITBY

One hundred and ninety-nine steps lead down from the majestic ruins of St Hilda's Abbey, perched high on the clifftop, into the old town of Whitby on the east bank of the River Esk. The East Bank is full of narrow cobbled streets and little alleyways while, on the other side of the river, the West Bank's quay shows that this is still a port and a fishing town. The two piers each have a lighthouse: a green light flashes from the west side and a red light from the east. Captain James Cook's statue stands on West Cliff: he set sail in the Whitby ship *Endeavour* to explore the seas and coasts of New Zealand and Australia.

LARPOOL RAILWAY VIADUCT

Just south of Whitby is the massive Larpool railway viaduct which spans the river Esk. It was part of the Scarborough to Whitby railway which opened in 1884 but fell victim to the Beeching cuts in the early 1960s. The viaduct is now the crowning glory of the 22-mile long footpath between the two seaside towns. For many holidaymakers crossing the viaduct by train was a sign that their holiday had just begun. The train from Scarborough would cross the viaduct, stop at West Cliff and then reverse down the steep incline into the town of Whitby.

ROBIN HOOD'S BAY

(above & right)

Some five miles (8km) south of Whitby
the red-roofed houses of Robin Hood's
Bay perch precariously on the cliffs and
seem to spill down to the sea wall. At
times the sea thunders up the street.

In 1536 Robin Hood's Bay was
recorded as a "fishing townlet of 50
boats". Around 350 years later 174
boats were registered here, making it
one of Yorkshire's largest fishing
communities. The origin of the name is
not clear – some say that the Abbot of
Whitby asked Robin Hood for help in
defending the shores against the
marauding Danish pirates. Later the
village was a haven for smugglers: tunnels
used to link many of the houses, and
contraband could reputedly be smuggled
from the water's edge to the top of the
hill without seeing the light of day.

The bay itself is edged by high
headlands known as North Cheek (also
called Ness Point) and South Cheek
(also known as the Old Peak). Erosion is
relentless: each year the North Sea eats
away about two inches from the cliffs.

RAVEN HALL HOTEL

(right and below)

At the southernmost end of the Esk valley, overlooking the glorious Robin Hood's Bay, lies the small village of Ravenscar and close by its twin village of Staintondale. The Cleveland Way national trail hugs the clifftop and gives splendid views; nearby, there is a National Trust coastal centre.

Raven Hall Country House Hotel, originally known as Peak House, which was built in 1774, stands on the site of a Roman hill fort. In 1788 Peak House was acquired by Dr Francis Willis, who numbered George III among his many illustrious patients. The King was rumoured to have been treated at Ravenscar during his bouts of insanity to avoid publicity.

Unfortunately Dr Willis was also an inveterate gambler, who was addicted to horse-racing - he particularly enjoyed the races at Doncaster. In the 1840s he is said to have lost the house when he bet on the slower of two woodlice running across a saucer.

SCARBOROUGH

High up on a promontory between Scarborough's two bays stands the castle, built early in the 12th century. In the Middle Ages, Scarborough Fair was held every year for 45 days from August 15, attracting traders, entertainers and customers from all over the country, even from Europe. The traditional song *Are you going to Scarborough Fair?* made the town famous again when recorded by Simon and Garfunkel in the 1960s.

The discovery of a mineral spring in 1620 led to the town's development as a spa. By 1660 physicians were recommending seabathing as a cure, which may make Scarborough the world's first seaside resort. As well as attracting royalty and other visitors for bathing and taking the waters, the town had a thriving harbour with tuna and herring fleets.

Today Scarborough boasts that it is the Queen of the Yorkshire coast. Its cultural life is vibrant: renowned playwright Sir Alan Ayckbourn has premiered nearly all of his 60-plus plays at the Stephen Joseph Theatre.

SCARBOROUGH CASTLE

The dramatic ruin of Scarborough Castle, perched on Castle Hill, dominates the town and harbour 300ft (90m) below. The first stone fortress was built here in the early 12th century by William le Gros; in the second half of the century, Henry II strengthened the curtain walls and destroyed the original gatehouse, erecting an elaborate three-storey square keep. Although the top of the keep has long since disappeared its ruin and many of the remaining walls show what an impressive structure the castle was. Scarborough Castle remained the strategically important northern base for kings and queens for almost five centuries and it was continually improved by various monarchs during this period. In later centuries the castle has had a colourful history – it was a casualty of the Civil War and during the First World War both town and castle were attacked by German battle cruisers. The building is now in the care of English Heritage.

FILEY

The most northerly town in the old East Riding of Yorkshire, Filey is a well-known holiday resort that lies on the shore between two valleys, Martin Ravine to the south and Church Ravine to the north. This small town started life as a fishing village, and developed into a fashionable resort in Victorian times when it was particularly popular with visitors who preferred its peace and quiet to the hubbub of Scarborough. The five-mile stretch of sand runs in an almost semi-circular sweep from Filey Brigg in the north to the 400ft (120m) high chalk cliffs of Speeton and Bempton in the south. The town's Edwardian festival, which celebrates the resort's heyday in the early part of the 20th century, was started in 1980 by enthusiastic local residents. The festival is an annual event in late June and pride of place goes to the festival parade.

Filey Brigg is a peninsula which protrudes out to sea for nearly a mile, forming a natural pier and breakwater. With its rocks covered in barnacles and mussels, it is one of the best places in Britain to spot unusual seabirds during the autumn, winter and spring.

BEMPTON CLIFFS *right & below*

Four miles' walk from Flamborough Head, the vertigo-inducing Bempton Cliffs rise to 400ft (120m). This chalk headland is considered the best place in England to see breeding seabirds, and the Royal Society for the Protection of Birds runs a nature reserve here. Between April and mid-August, visitors have close-up views of puffins, gannets, guillemots, razorbills, kittiwakes and fulmars as they nest and breed. In recent years the decline in sand eels in this part of the North Sea has led to a drastic reduction in the numbers of chicks successfully raised by kittiwakes.

FLAMBOROUGH HEAD *(above and left)*

Just north of Bridlington this stunning promontory extends six miles (9.5km) out into the North Sea. It is the most northern chalk cliff in Britain, rising 178ft (54m) up from the sea. The action of the waves over the centuries has produced a fantastic shape, with beautiful coves and sea caves. The lighthouse was built in 1806. Further back stands the old beacon light tower built in the 1670s, though it is possible that no fire was ever lit here to warn sailors of the dangerous rocks below. Many ships came to grief here, including the flagship of the newly independent US navy in the Battle of Flamborough Head, a humiliating defeat for the British Navy during the American Revolutionary War in 1779.

BRIDLINGTON

Today tourism is Bridlington's principal business – its two glorious sandy beaches have received the accolade of having "the best sand in the UK for sculpting and building sandcastles". The town's busy harbour is also a prime tourist attraction - there are working fishing boats and pleasure craft which offer cruises along the spectacular heritage coastline. Bridlington has a long history - in the Domesday Book, compiled in 1086, the settlement was called Bretlington. By the 19th century it was known locally as Burlington, although the government insisted it was Bridlington.

AN HISTORIC TOWN

Once two separate towns, the old town of Bridlington, about a mile from the sea, has now merged with Bridlington Quay, the historic port area. The South Pier and the harbour were completed in the middle of the 19th century and the resort soon attracted thousands of visitors during the summer months. Until this time, the port had been famous for shipbuilding and the export of grain. These soon disappeared when the railway was built, opening up the Yorkshire coast to holidaymakers. A famous 19th-century visitor was Charlotte Brontë, who visited her great friend Ellen Nussey at Easton House in 1839, and later wrote enthusiastically to her friends about the glories of the sea here. Bridlington is thought to have been the model for the town of Bretton in her novel *Villette*.

KINGSTON UPON HULL

Hull is a modern, vibrant city which stands at the confluence of the rivers Hull and Humber. Its centre is largely a product of the years since the Second World War, when more than 90 per cent of the houses were damaged by bombs. Hull's history and rich maritime heritage reach far back to Saxon times, when it was known as Wyke-upon-Hull. You can still wander the old town's narrow cobbled lanes in the footsteps of William Wilberforce, the great reformer who fought for the abolition of slavery, and was born here in 1759. Traditionally Hull traded with the Continent, never joining the slave trade, and so its citizens supported Wilberforce's campaign.

AQUARIUM

The poet Philip Larkin, a long-term resident of Hull and librarian at the university, declared, "Hull is a city with a lot of sky". This is particularly so down by the water's edge. On Sammy's Point, where the river Hull meets the Humber Estuary, is the world's only "submarium", known as The Deep. Europe's deepest aquarium, it contains a staggering 2.5 million litres of water and 87 tonnes of salt. This millennium project combines a major tourist attraction with a world-class marine research facility, run by Hull University. The World Ocean Discovery Centre's brief is to research all the planet's oceans, seas and marine animals.

HULL DOCKS

For over 700 years Hull has been a major European port. In the recent past it was also a centre for deep sea fishing but this has been in decline since the "Cod Wars" of the 70s. Today it is still one of Britain's busiest ports and business is booming. More than 10m tonnes of freight and 1m passengers pass through the docks every year. Down on King George Dock you will find sleek superferries that sail daily to and from Zeebrugge and Rotterdam. Some of the older shipping docks have been given a new purpose. Two now form the marina, with yachts and other boats, while another, Princes Dock, has been transformed into Princes Quay, a giant glass shopping complex built on stilts over the water. Just a stone's throw away, the cobbled streets of the old town and an indoor market ensure that there is still a link to the past.

THE CITY CENTRE

Hull has the unenviable reputation of being the most bombed town in the United Kingdom during the Second World War. More than 95% of property in the city was damaged and most of the centre was destroyed. The town and the docks were used as a practise run by enemy pilots and as a reprisal for the Allied bombing of Hamburg. In one raid all of the city's department stores were wiped out. The photograph above shows the city centre and in the foreground, Queen's Gardens, Queen Victoria Square and the distinctive triangular-shaped Hull Maritime Museum.

HUMBER BRIDGE

The huge Humber Estuary drains about one-fifth of England's total land area. For centuries the communities on either side of the estuary were a world away from each other. Hull's thriving docks to the north were a 50 mile (80km) drive away for the businesses in Grimsby to the south. All this changed in 1981 when, after nine years under construction, the world's third longest single span suspension bridge was opened to traffic, linking Barton on the south bank with Hessle in the north. By 2032 it is expected that the toll paid by vehicles crossing will have paid off the cost of construction. The bridge (1.4 miles/2,220m long) has a centre span of 1541 yards (1,410m). If you unravelled the wire used in the suspension cables you could almost circle the Earth twice over.

GOOLE

The word *goole* is derived from the Anglo-Saxon, and it means "outlet to a river". Goole today is a bustling inland port, sometimes called the Port in Green Fields, a reference to the beautiful countryside that surrounds the town. It sits about 50 miles (80km) from the open sea, on the confluence of the Don and the Ouse, two tributaries of the river Humber. Before the Humber Bridge was built, Goole was the main crossing point for drivers wanting to reach the other side of the river. A Dutch engineer in the early 1600s built a canal system to link nearby coalfields with the tidal water. In 1826 the Aire & Calder Navigation Company built a canal from Leeds to Goole and a large town developed exporting coal from the West Riding of Yorkshire to the Continent. Vessels known as "Tom Puddings" (compartment boats from the canals) would unload directly into coal ships here. A few decades later, when the railway arrived, the town rapidly expanded and experienced a boom. At its peak in the late 19th century Goole rivalled Hull and there were passenger ferry services to Europe together with a large shipyard, which was sited across the river in Old Goole. Unlike its neighbour, Goole was only bombed once in the Second World War by a lost German plane trying to find Leeds.

SPURN HEAD

This narrow spit arches across the mouth of the river Humber and forms the southernmost point of the Yorkshire coast. It is an easy drive on the A1033 and then the B1445 to Easington. The spit lies 16km south-east of Withernsea and 40km east of Hull. Its sand and shingle stretch for three and a half miles (5.5km) out to Spurn Point which can be seen in the photograph.

In the 18th and 19th centuries whaling ships from Hull would load shingle onto their boats from the spit to use as ballast, which would make the ships more stable as they sailed to the whaling grounds of the North Atlantic; at its peak they were taking 500,000 tonnes a year. The ballast was dumped at sea as the whalers filled their holds with whalemeat before the voyage home. Over the years, this loss led to increased erosion of the spit by strong gales. The Victorians began some sea defence work which was continued by the Ministry of Defence; in the 1950s the Yorkshire Wildlife Trust took over this fragile spit of land. Today Spurn Point is a National Nature Reserve and an interesting place to visit, as its unique environment supports a wide range of moths, butterflies and birds.

There have been lighthouses on Spurn for more than 500 years. The distinctive black and white lighthouse that can be seen in the photograph was built in 1885; a century later, in 1985, it was replaced by the modern technology of smaller lights at the very end of the point. Since 1810 the Humber lifeboat has been stationed at Spurn Point. Its importance is demonstrated by the fact that it is the UK's only lifeboat with a full crew of paid employees. The crew of seven men and their families live in houses close by the station.

Published in 2011 by Myriad Books Limited
35 Bishopsthorpe Road, London SE26 4PA

Photographs copyright © Flight Images
Text copyright © Lisa Pritchard
Lisa Pritchard has asserted her right under the
Copyright, Designs and Patents Act 1998 to be identified
as the author of this work. All rights reserved. No part
of this publication may be reproduced, stored
on a retrieval system, or transmitted in any form or by
any means, electronic, mechanical, photocopying,
recording or otherwise, without the prior permission
of the copyright owners.

ISBN 1 84746 237 5

Designed by Jerry Goldie Graphic Design

Printed in China

www.myriadbooks.com